# ELEMENTS

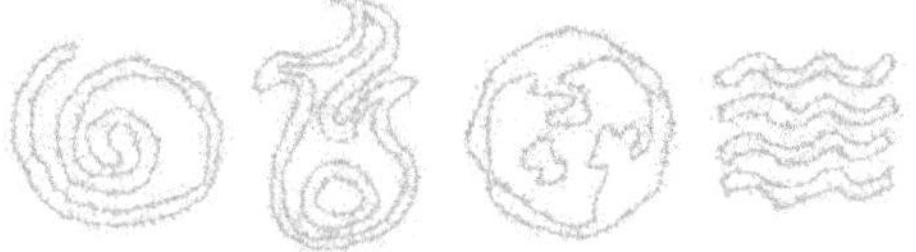

# ELEMENTS

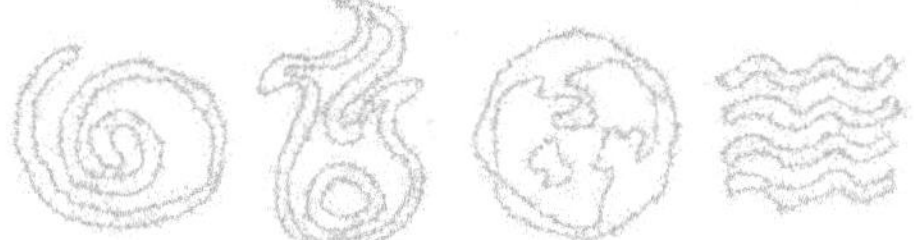

## poetry and images

Chuck Alen

ELEMENTS
poetry and images




ISBN: 979-8-9937366-0-0 (Paperback Edition)

Cover/Illustrations: Chuck Alen


Published by Waking Tree
www.wakingtree.com

*To Melissa*
*Thank you for your love and support*
*You make me a better human*

# Contents

# Introduction

Ever since the concept of the four elements sprung forth millennia ago with help from the likes of Aristotle and the Chinese creators of the I-Ching, humans have been captivated by this prophetic framework.

Following this inception, these four elements of air, fire, earth, and water have been used while searchers grasped for essential truth in areas ranging from physical science and philosophy to spirituality and even emotional states.

This book of poetry and companion artwork explores the spirit and varied interpretations of these four classical elements.

# AIR

the breath

of connection

can sneak up on you

bringing divine clarity

through expansion

to all that is

of air

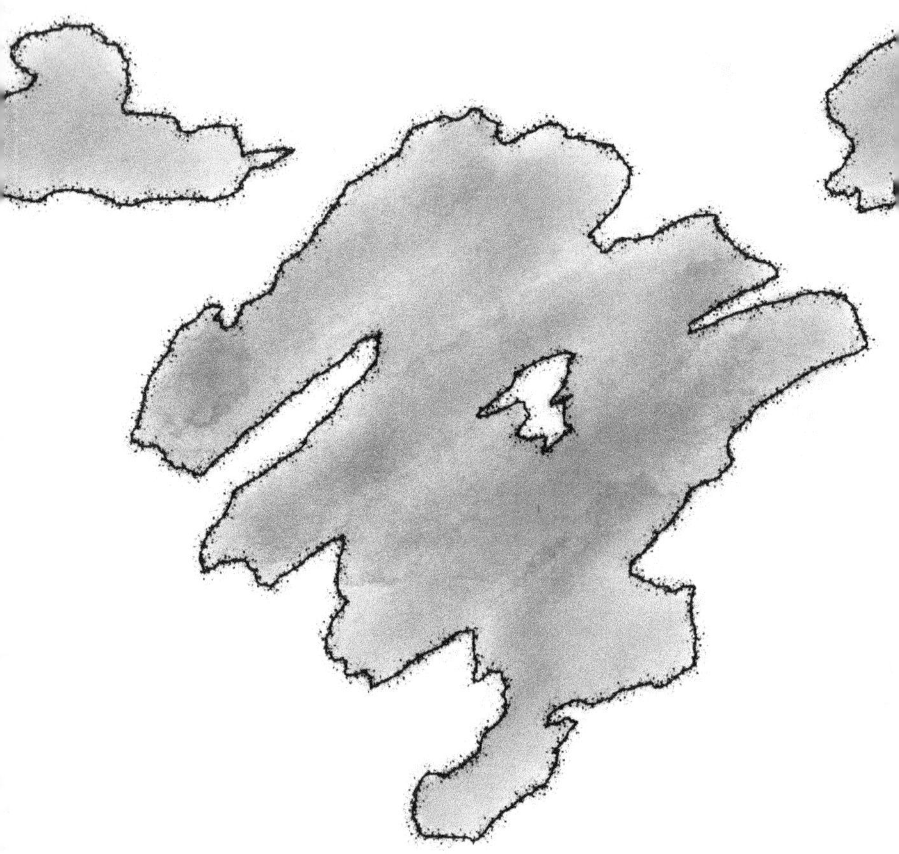

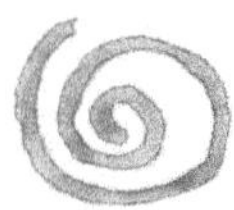

connect to it all

transcend beyond everything

let it transform you

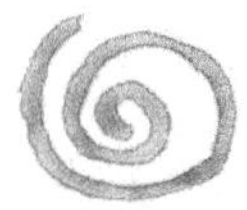

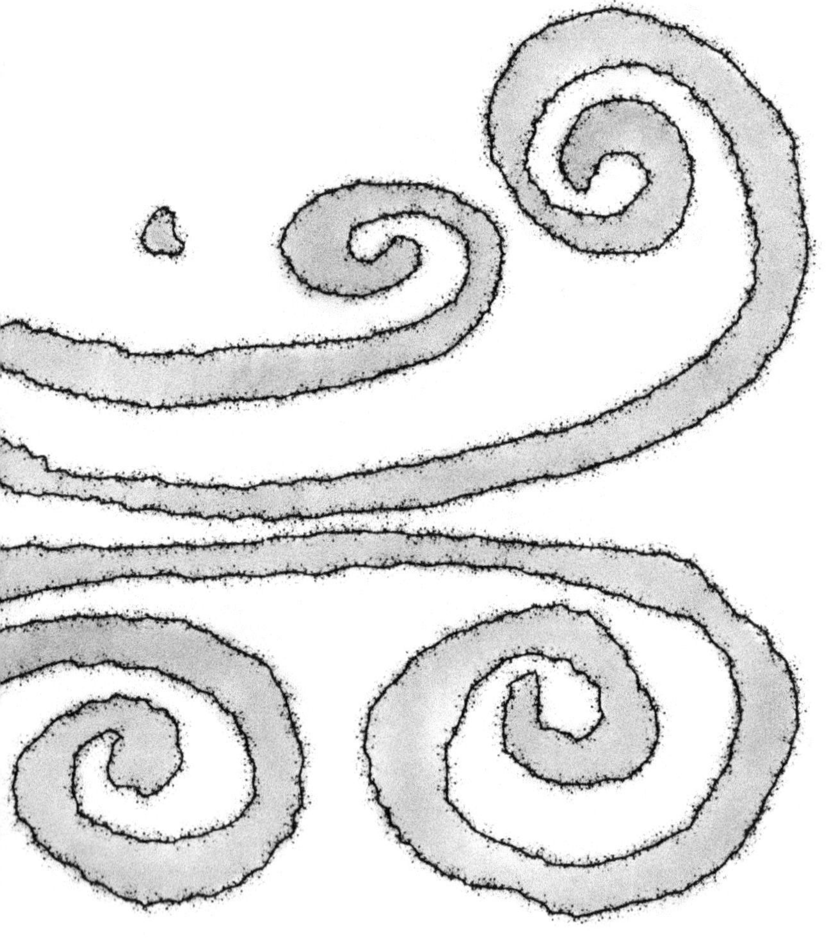

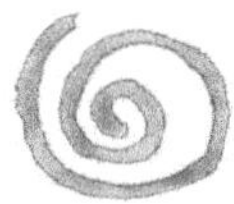

there are shapes that bind

but freedom is inherent

you can ride the wind

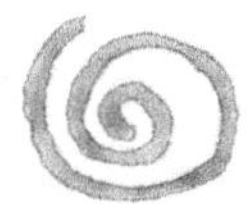

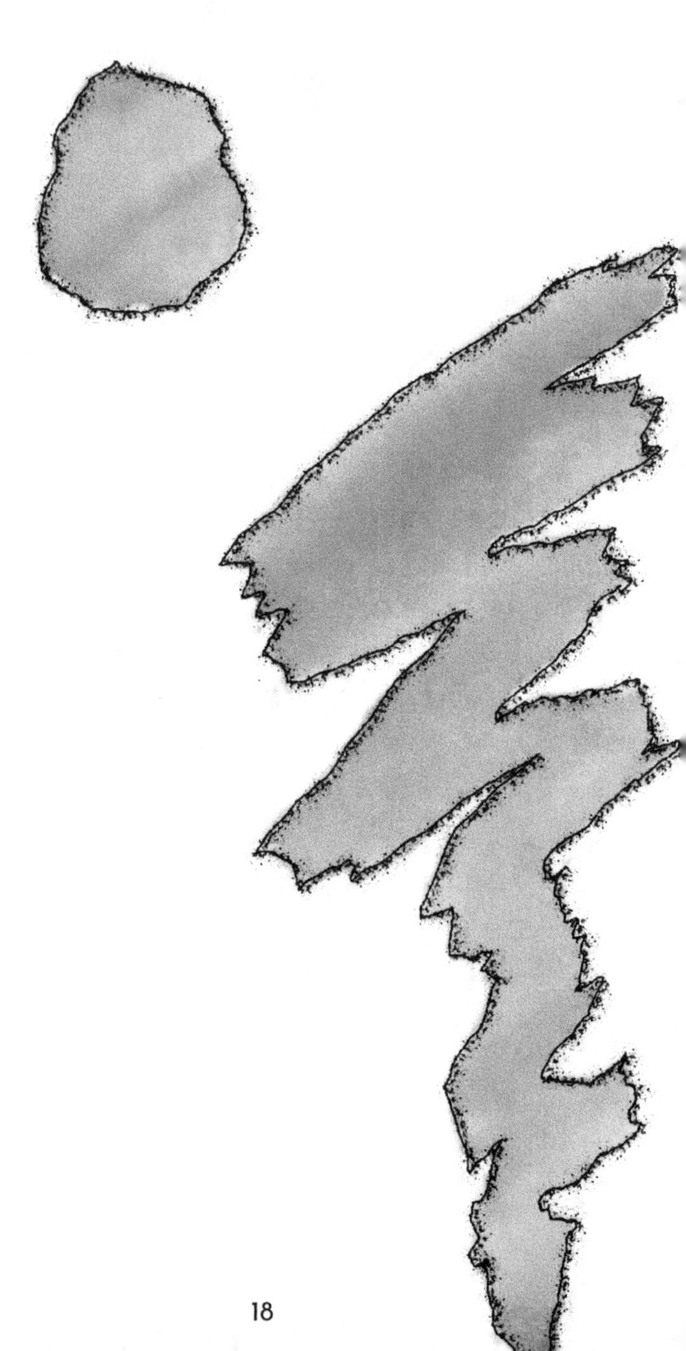

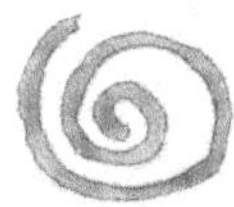

allow freedom now

do not let the height scare you

you will soar above

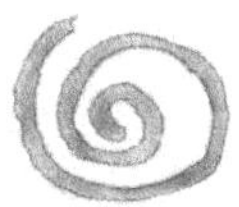

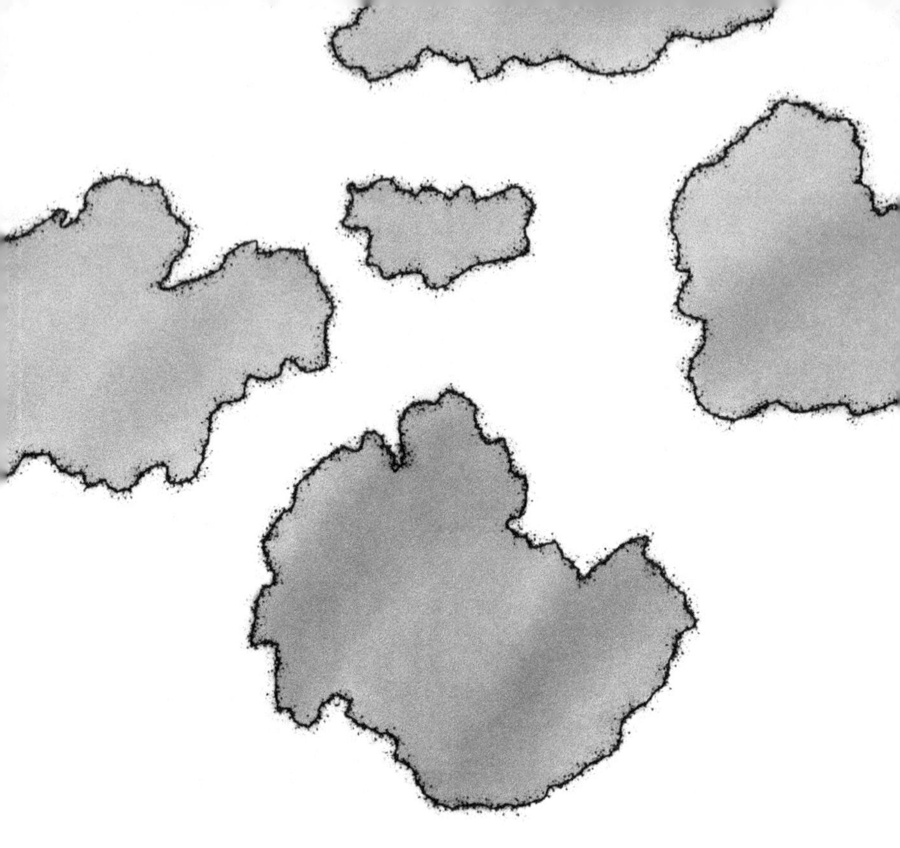

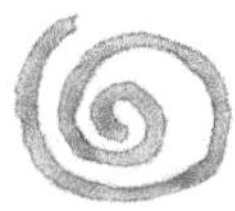

let the clouds float high

the sky need not be empty

the sun is still there

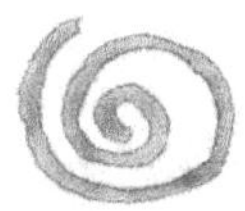

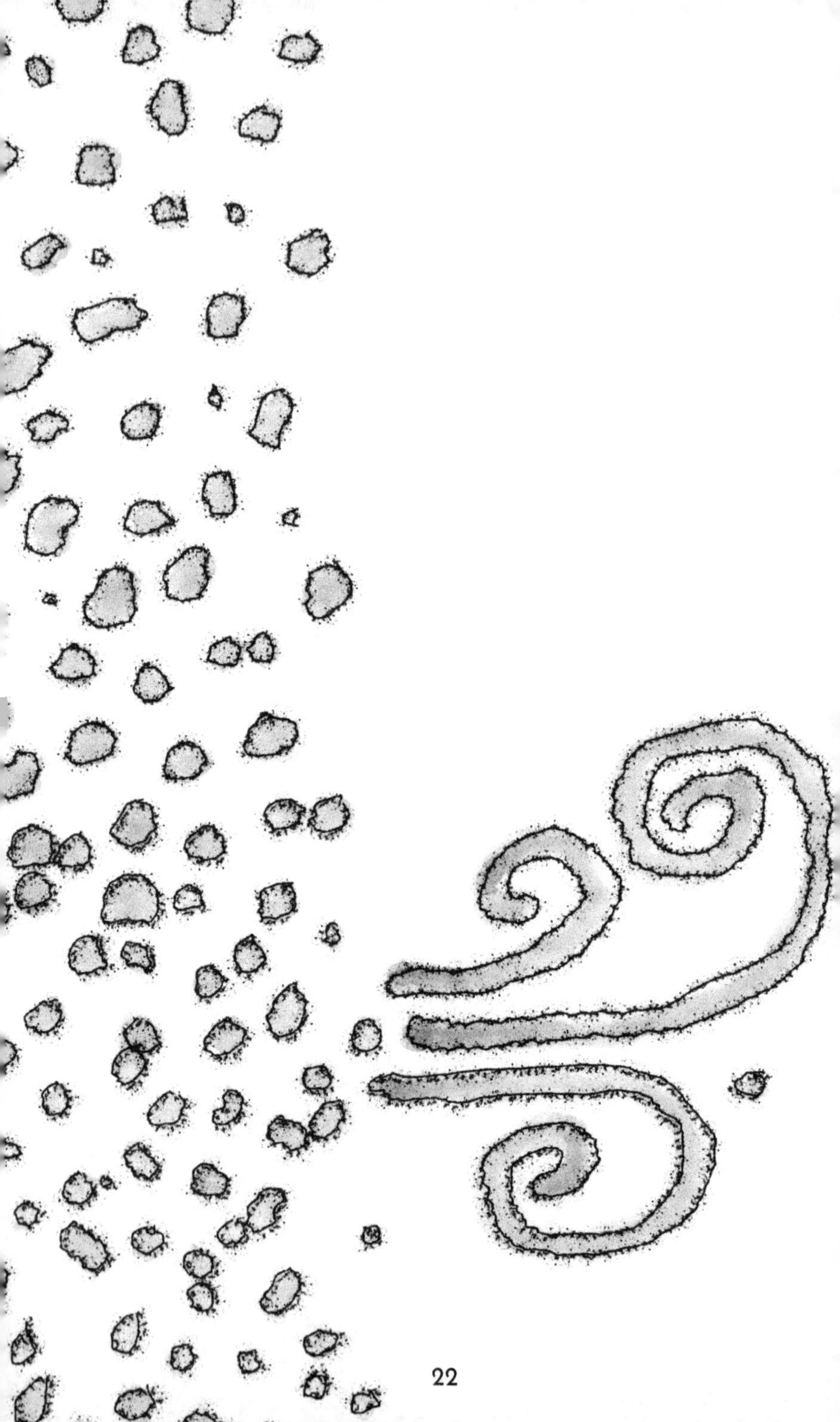

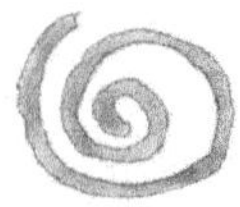

a collective breath

singular exhalation

return of spirit

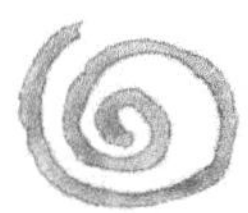

# FIRE

rising

from the ashes

transform your being

moving it beyond

the possible to

the probable

of fire

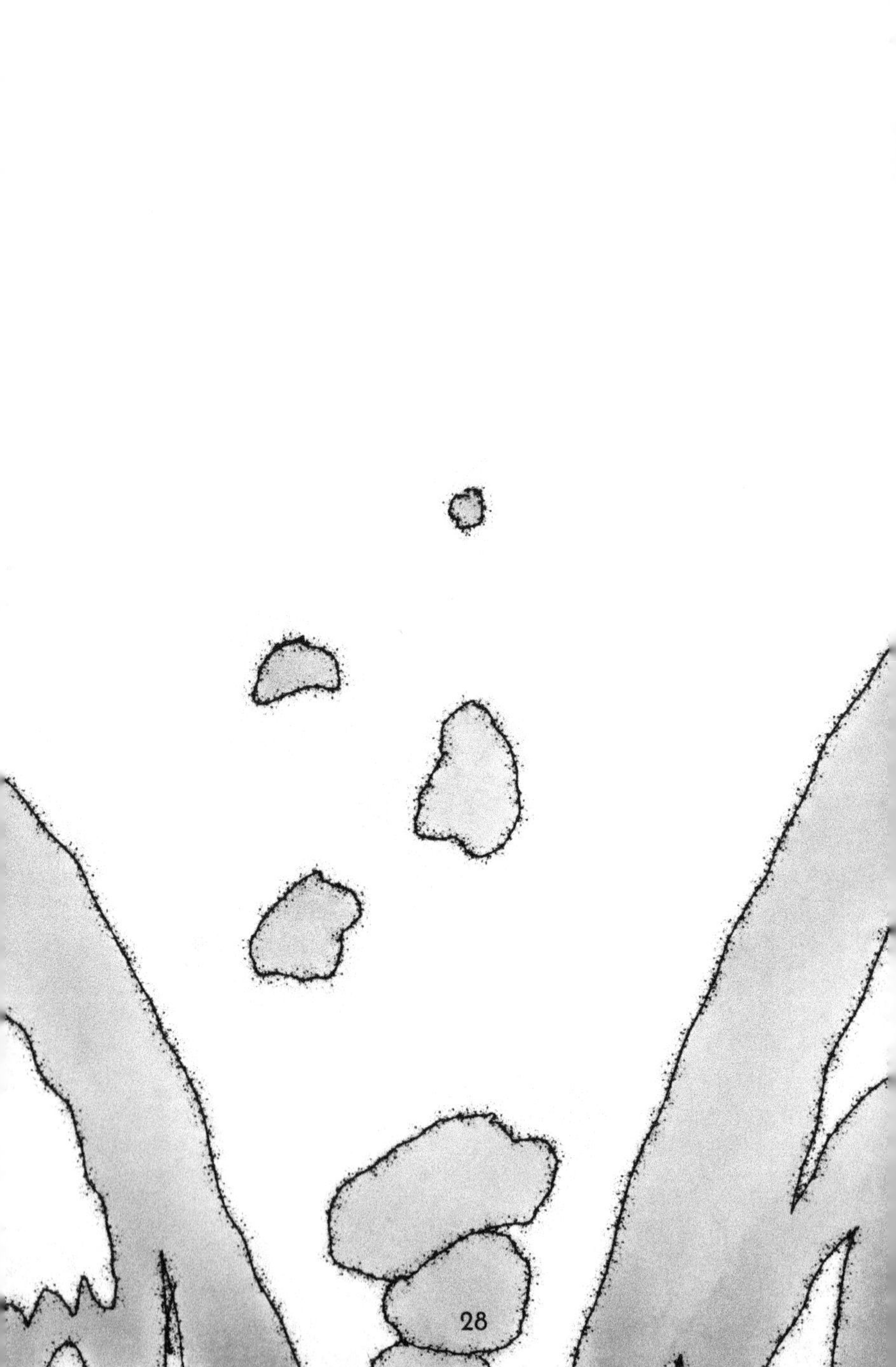

28

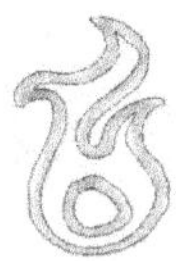

emerge from the dark

it is all an illusion

walk free from shadow

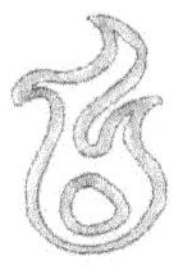

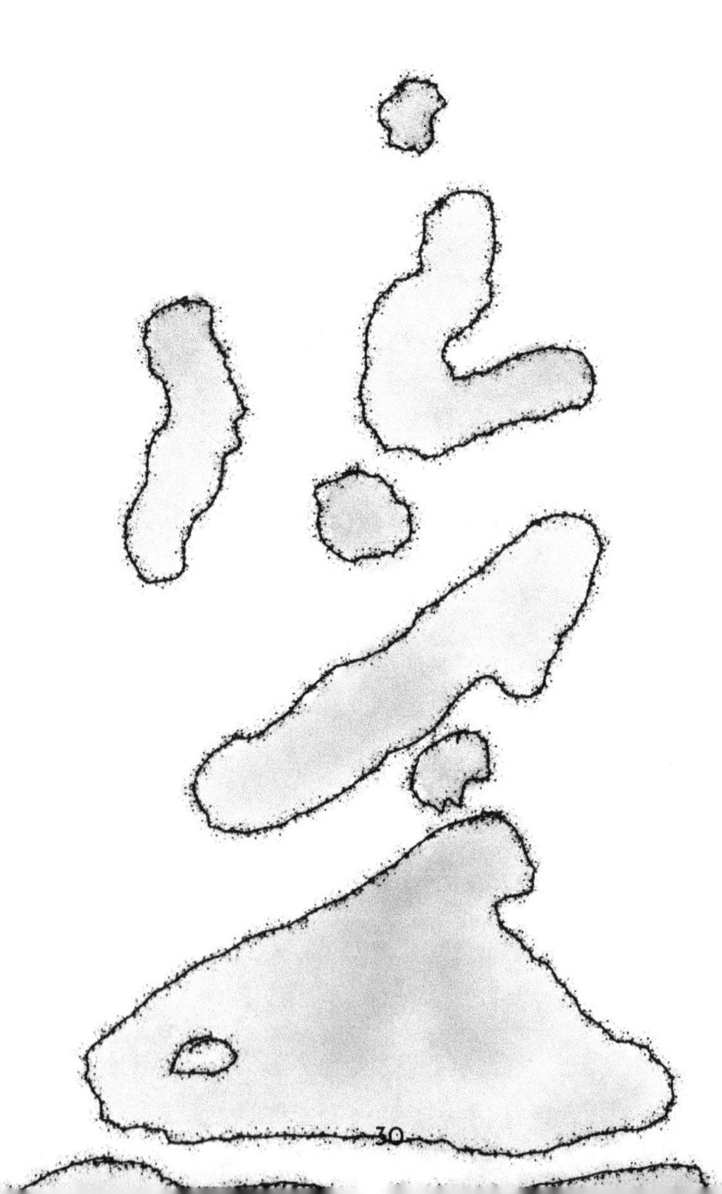

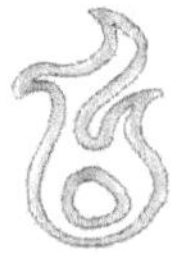

warm your hands my friend

the embers are there for you

no need for the flame

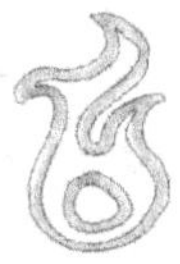

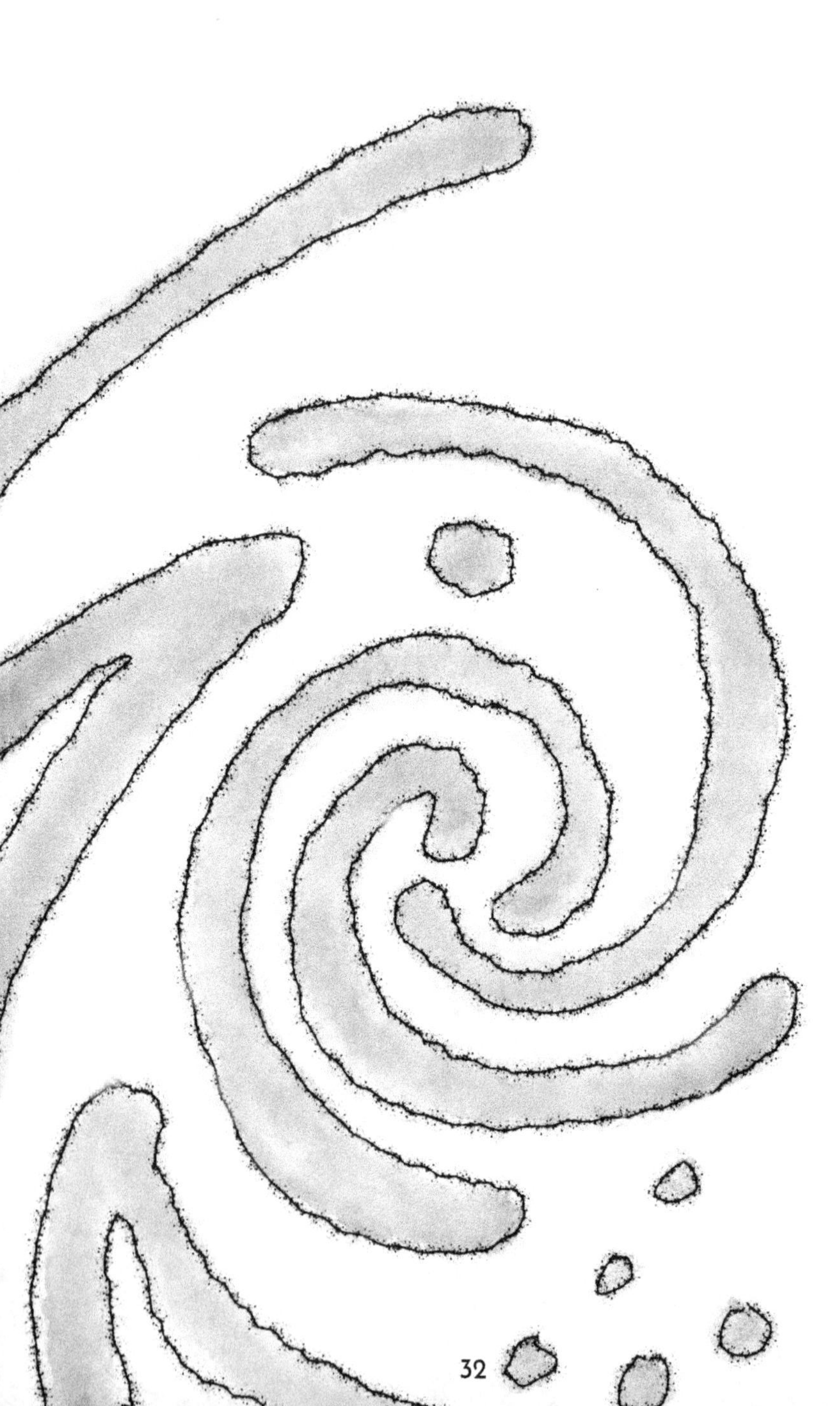

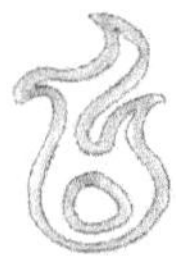

don't let anger flow

restrain the impulse to act

reflection is key

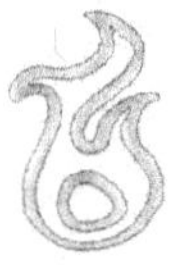

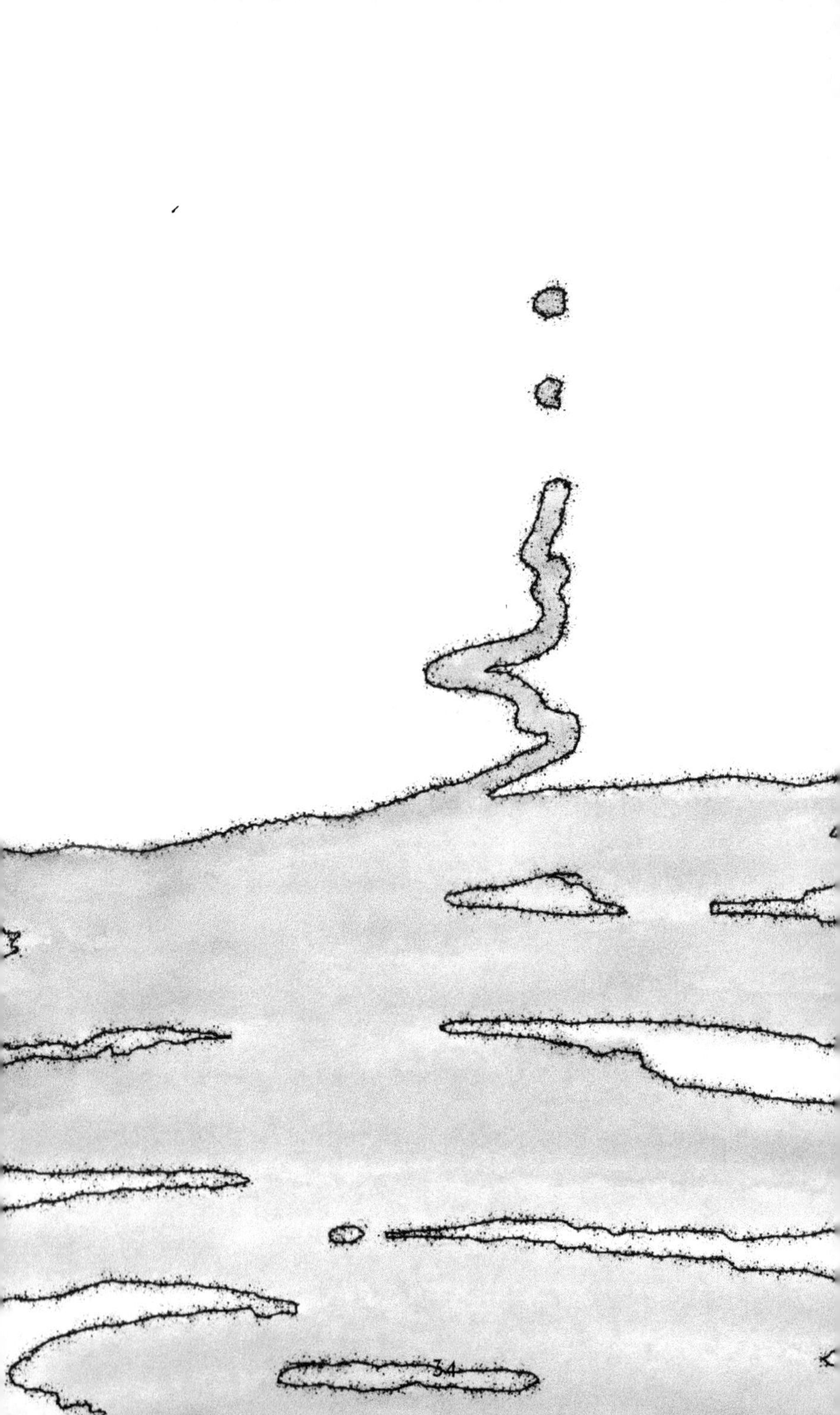

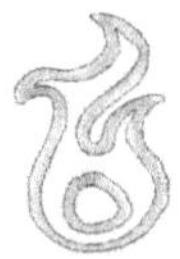

burn all of it down

allow this space for regrowth

birth needs the absence

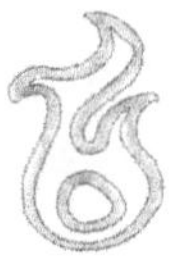

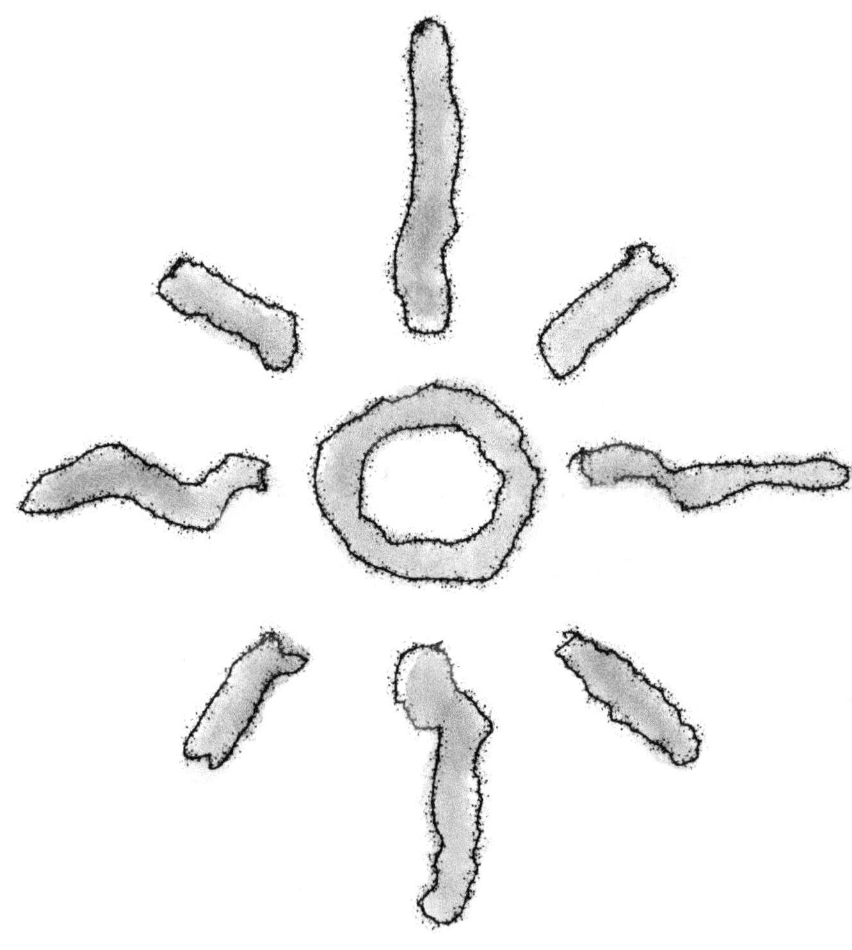

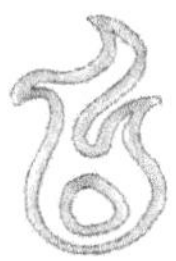

the rays from the sun

dance upon the earth's surface

bringing light and life

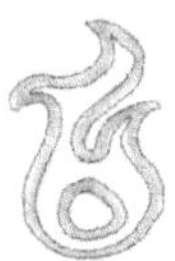

# EARTH

root yourself

in the present and

what has always been

this foundation

allows for patience

and balance

to overtake

you

of earth

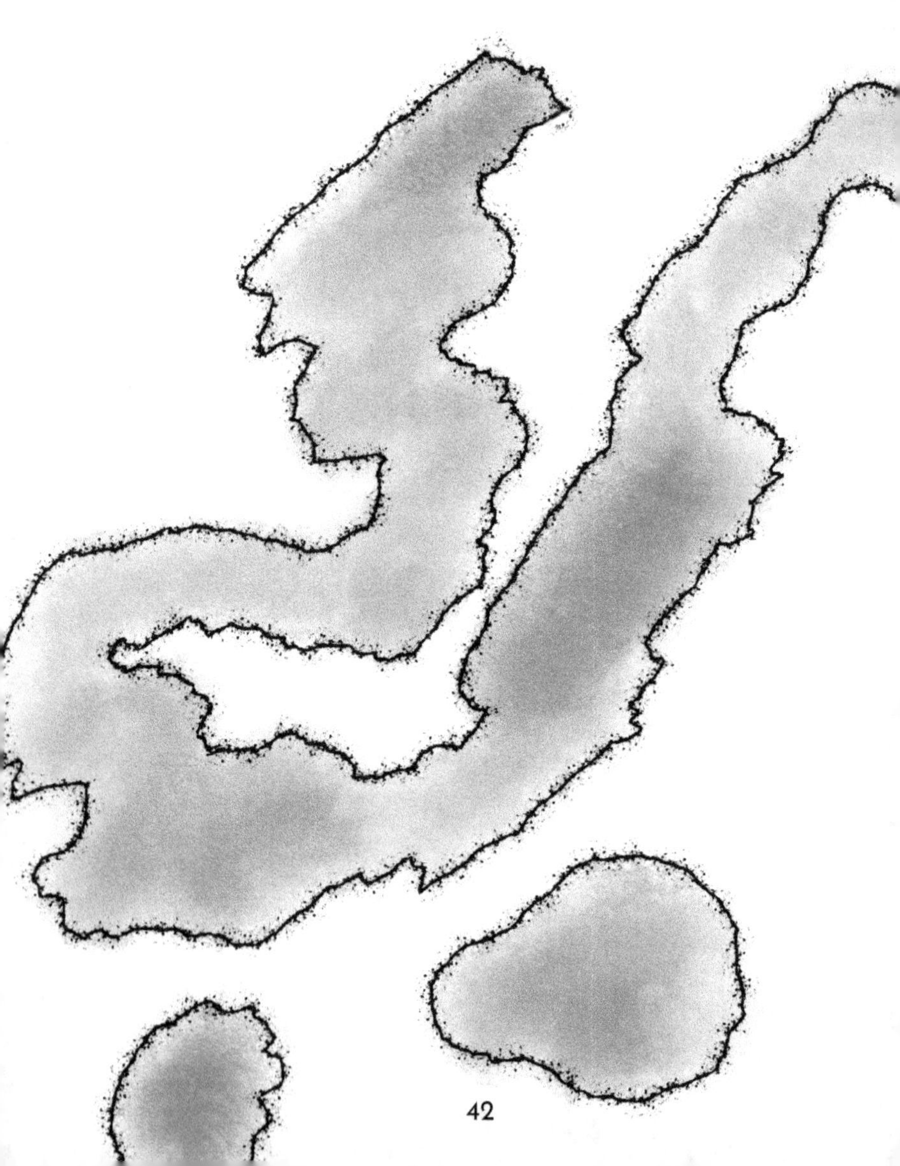

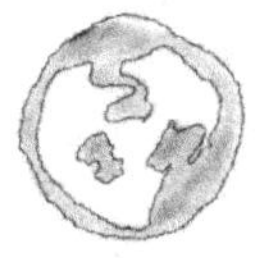

keep your feet below

and look for that which is true

or you shall rise down

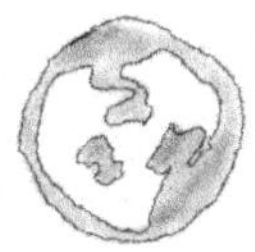

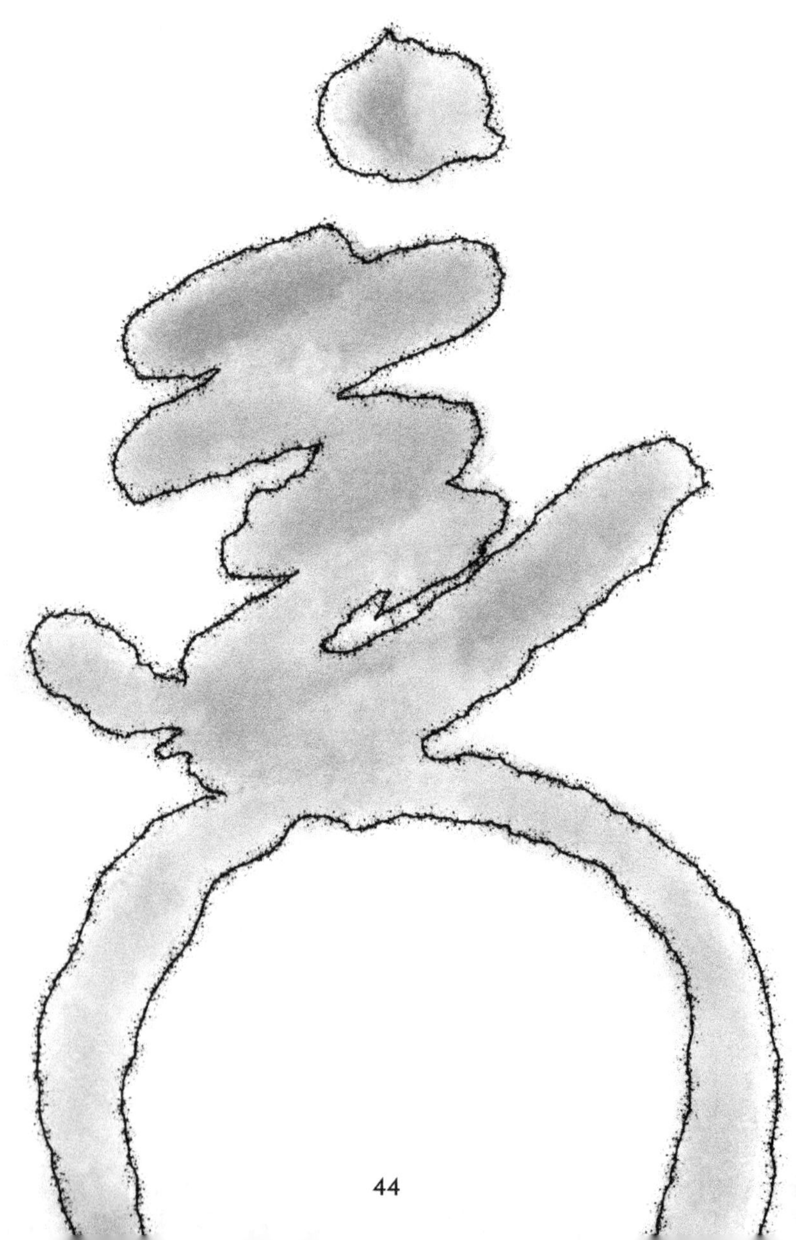

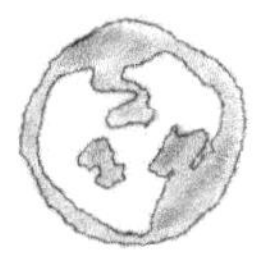

allow for patience

connect to the source of things

the lessons are real

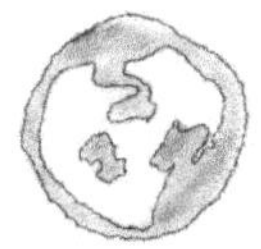

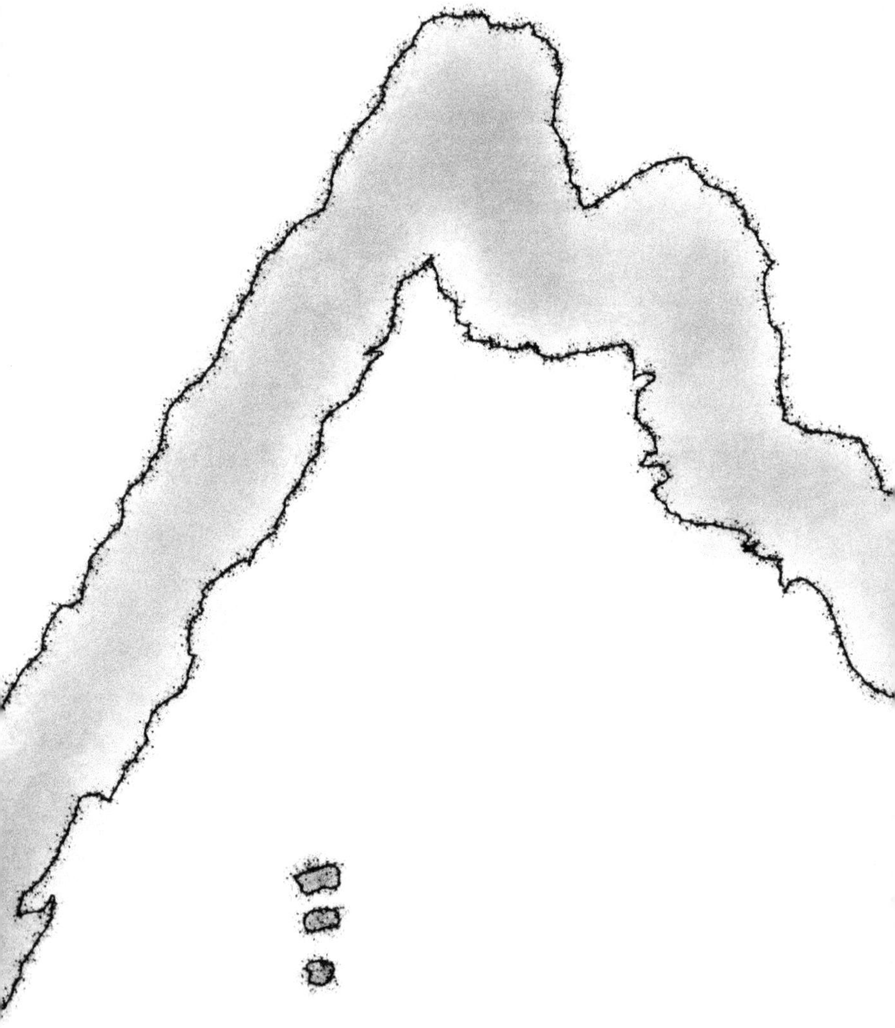

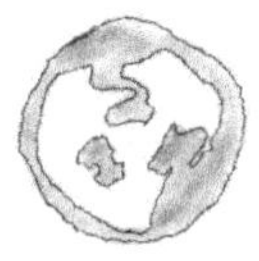

the mountain will not

neither will the great valley

you must move to them

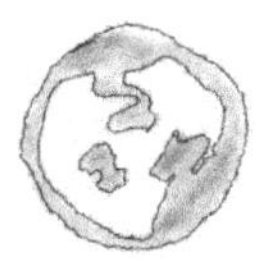

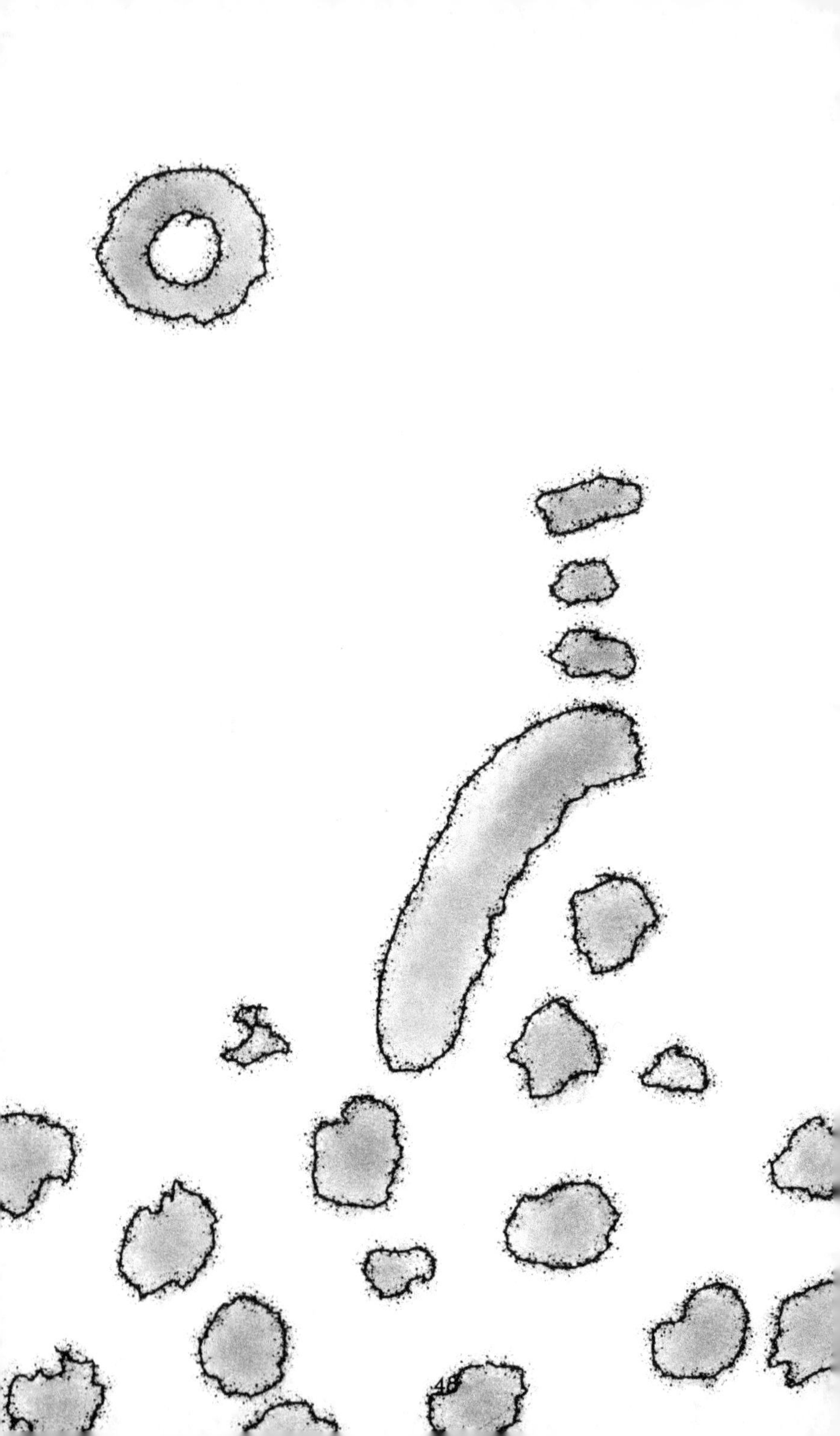

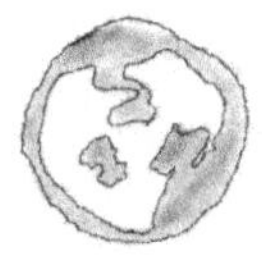

nurture what is good

relinquish all of the bad

step into the light

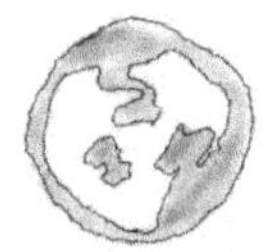

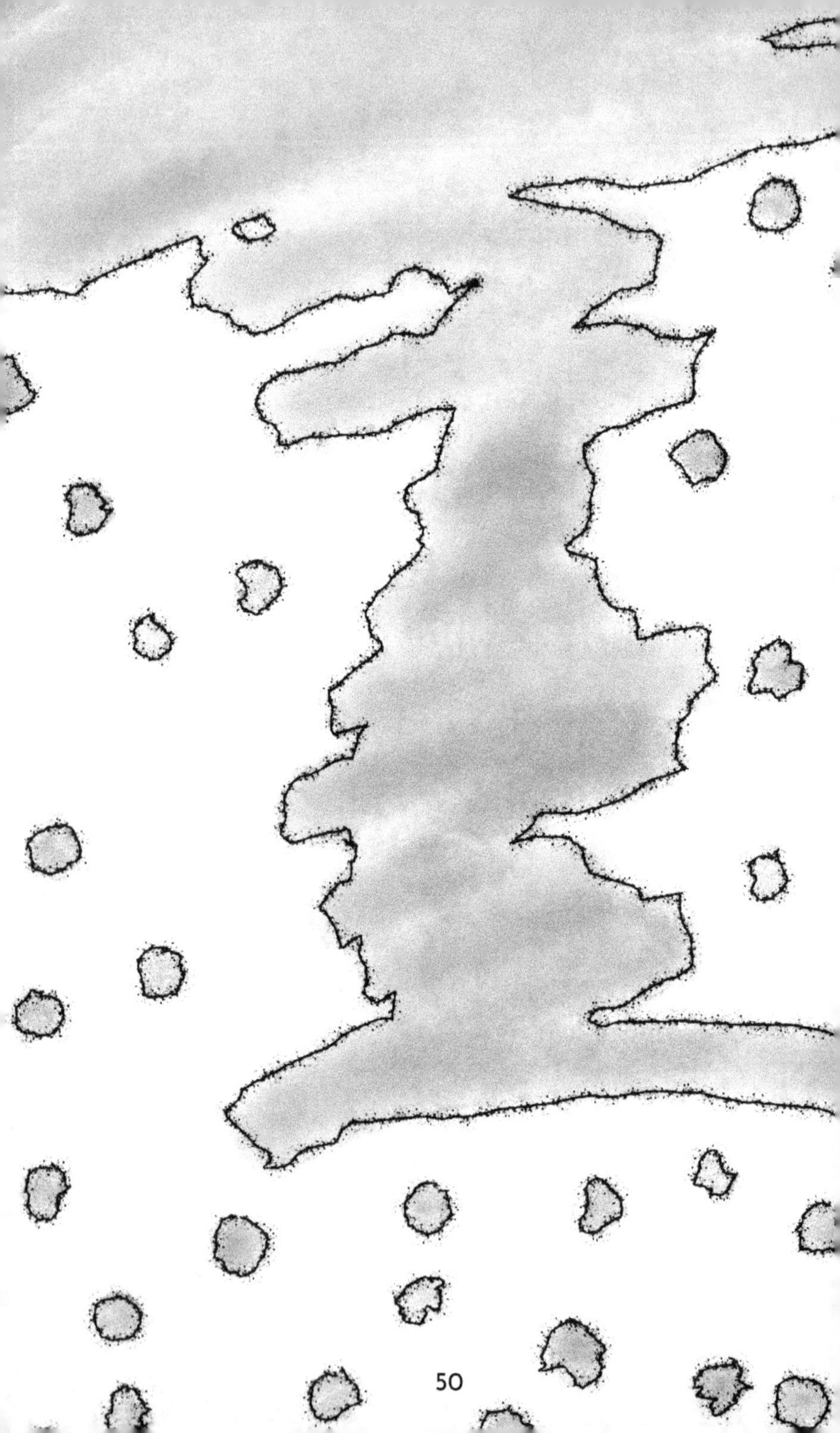

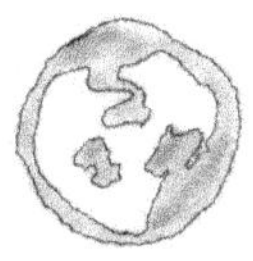

the leaves fall today

they rejoin the mother now

feeding all to come

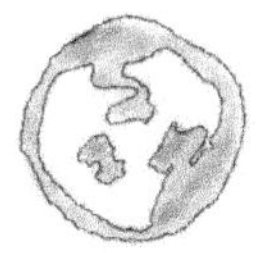

# WATER

let it flow

purify your being

allowing a renewed

connection between

the individual

and

collective

of water

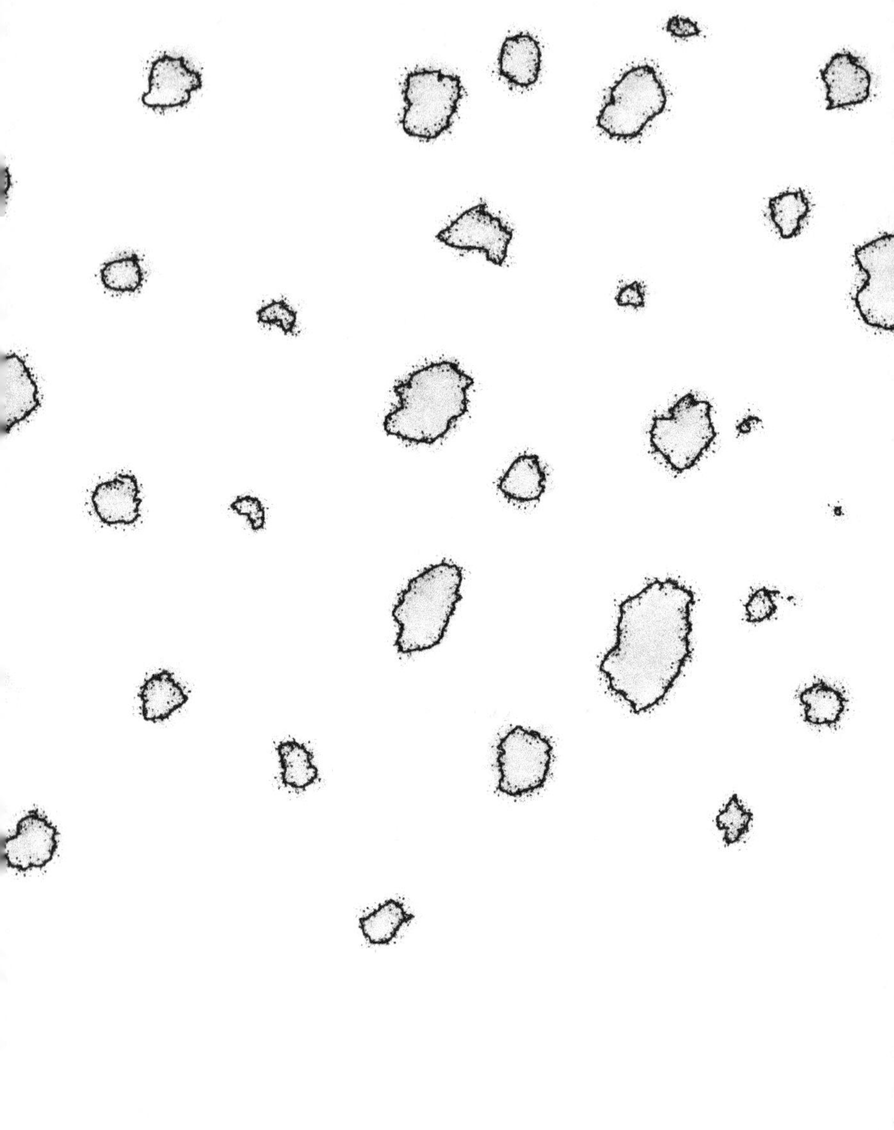

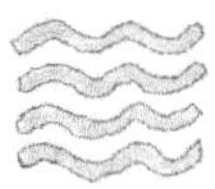

still like a mirror

the winter falls upon all

to end the cycle

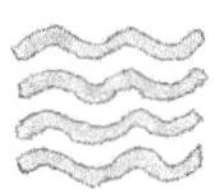

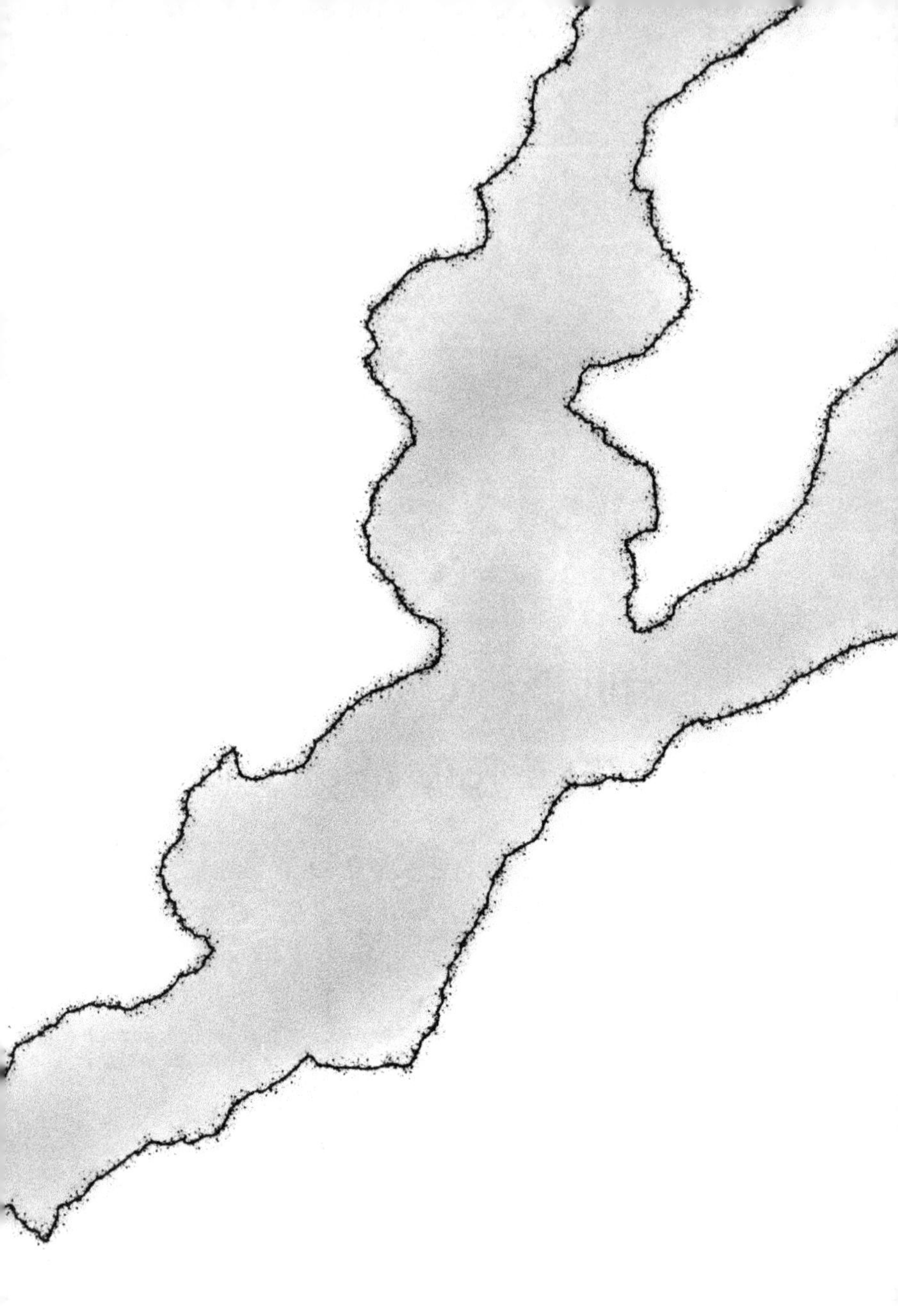

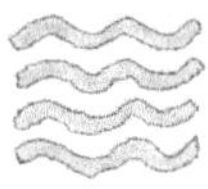

the river flows past

bringing the favors you ask

to some place unknown

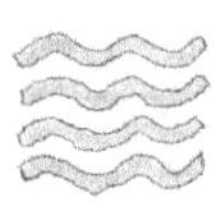

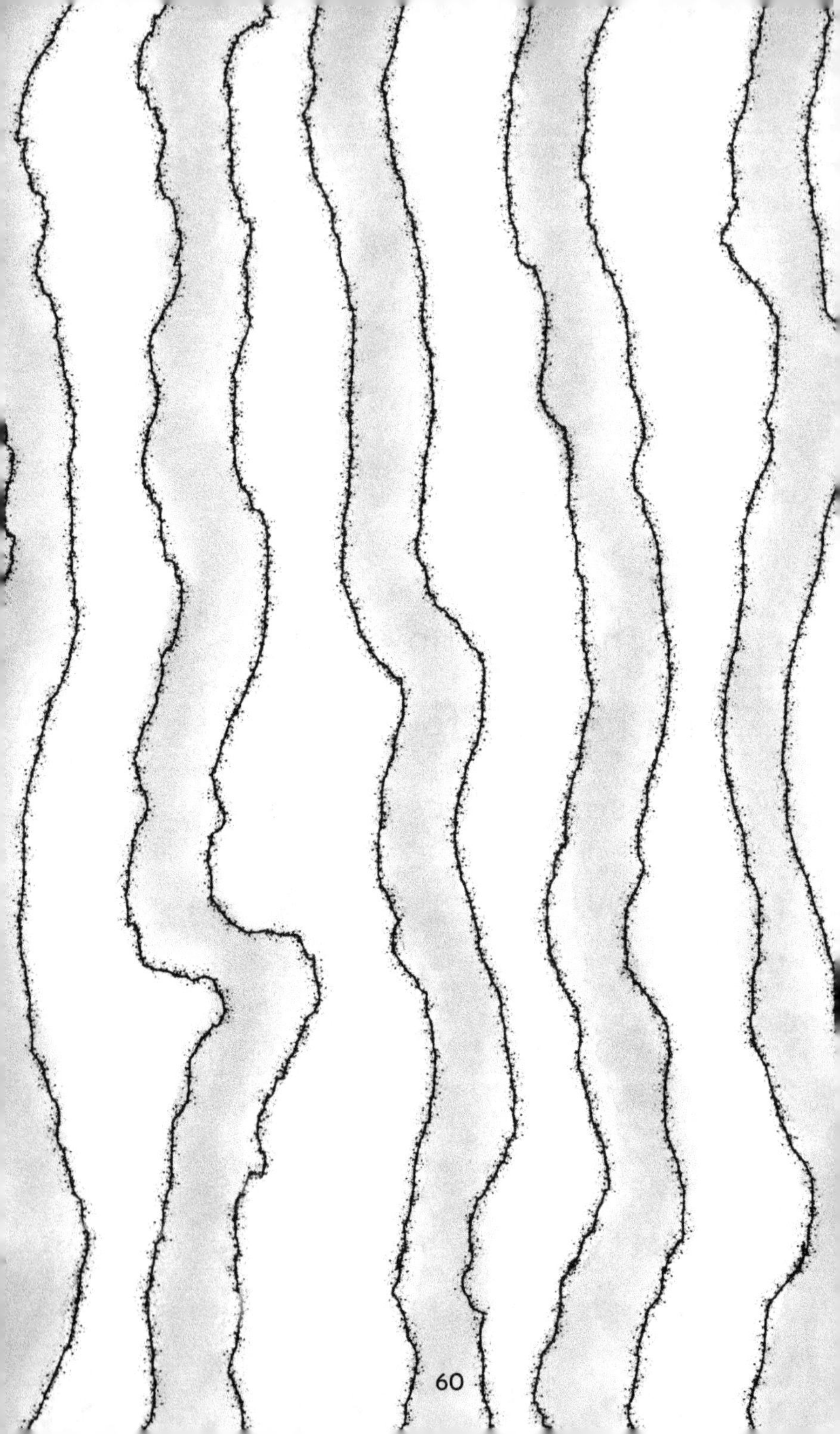

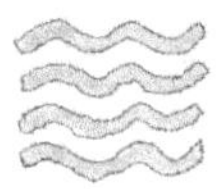

boundless emptiness

an everlasting fullness

it all is the same

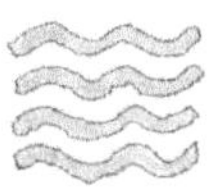

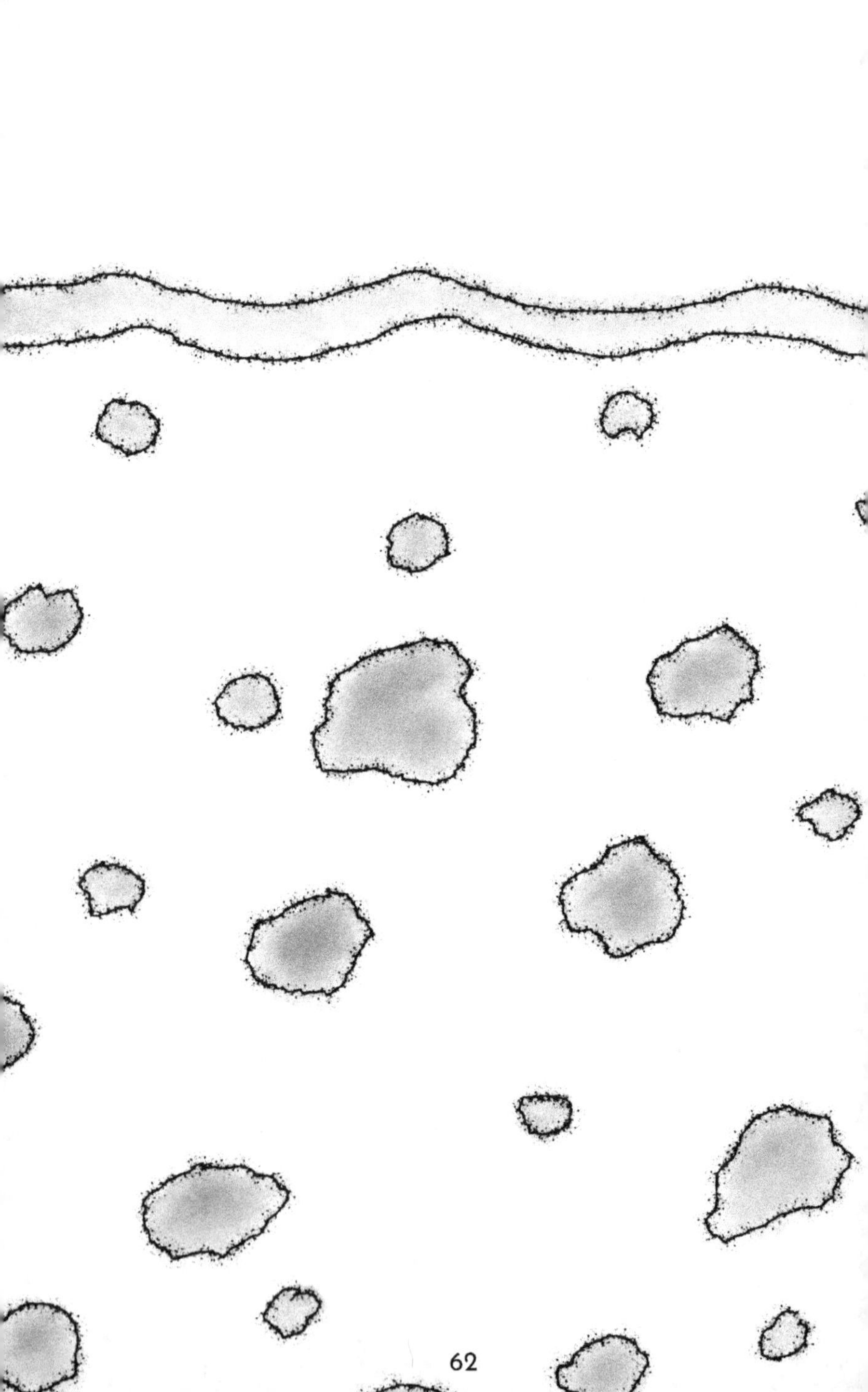

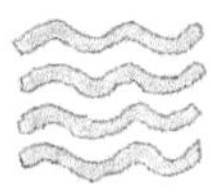

we float here today

waiting for a sign of peace

or maybe to drown

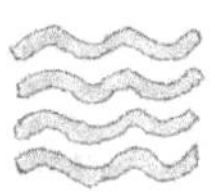

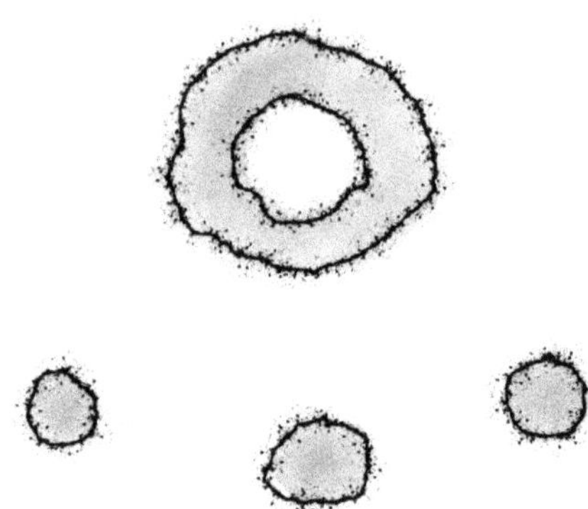

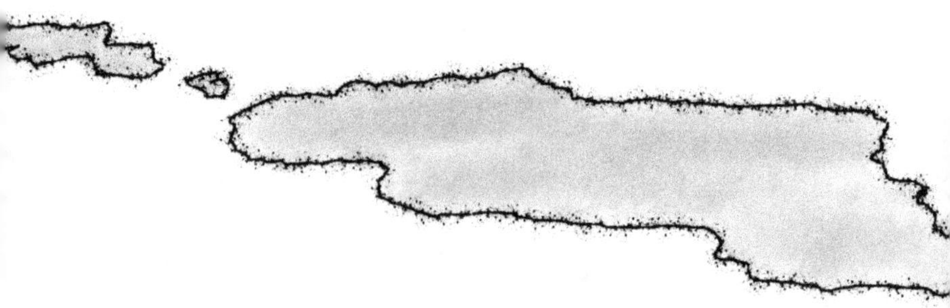

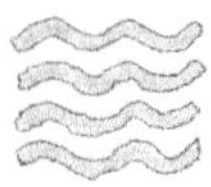

dry puddles wait here

for the sky to cry again

yearning for sadness

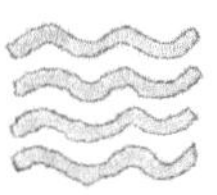

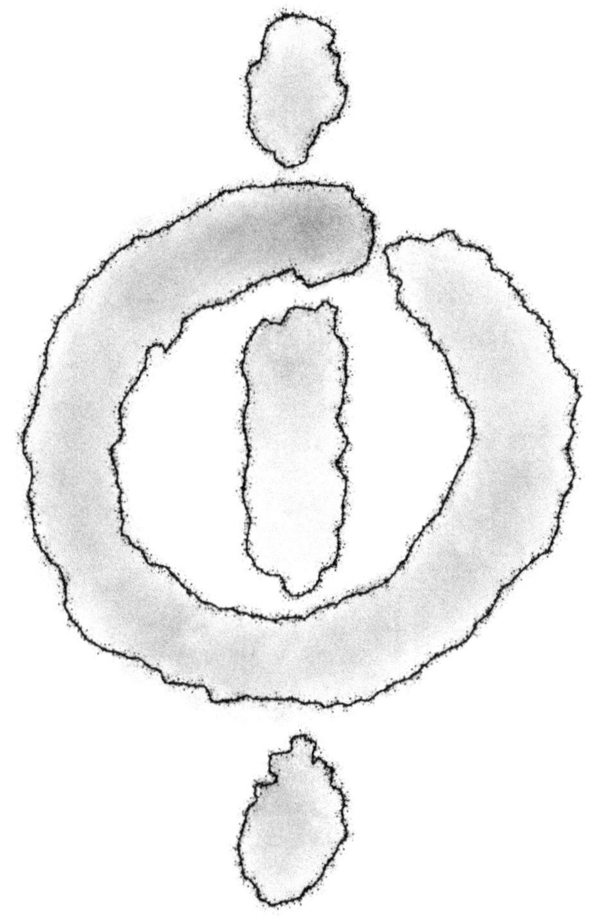

# About the Author

Chuck Alen is a quasi-optimistic curmudgeon attempting to provide benefit to humanity in some modest way through random philosophizing, the written word, visual art, and sometimes even musical endeavors.

*for more info:*
*www.chuckalen.com*

9 798993 736600